Spirituals
for Choirs

20 specially commissioned choral arrangements

Compiled and edited by

Bob Chilcott

MUSIC DEPARTMENT

OXFORD
UNIVERSITY PRESS

OXFORD
UNIVERSITY PRESS

Great Clarendon Street, Oxford OX2 6DP, England
198 Madison Avenue, New York, NY10016, USA

Oxford University Press is a department of the University of Oxford.
It furthers the University's aim of excellence in research, scholarship,
and education by publishing worldwide

Oxford is a registered trade mark of Oxford University Press
in the UK and in certain other countries

© Oxford University Press 2001

The moral rights of the author have been asserted

Database right Oxford University Press (maker)

First published 2001

1 3 5 7 9 10 8 6 4 2

ISBN 0–19–343537–3

Music and text origination by
Barnes Music Engraving Ltd., East Sussex
Printed in Great Britain on acid-free paper by
Halstan & Co. Ltd., Amersham, Bucks.

CONTENTS

Spirituals
for Choirs

Almost all choral singers world-wide have sung spirituals regularly in their choir life and, for many choir directors, they form an essential part of their programming. From my own time as a singer at King's College, Cambridge and with the King's Singers, I have found that to sing spirituals is a liberating experience. The joy, the anguish, and the beauty found in the words and music communicate immediately, not only to the singer but also to the listener. The songs seem timeless and speak to all people.

In this collection of 20 new arrangements, the aim is to encourage a fresh look at these wonderful songs. Many of them will be well known to most singers, and some will be entirely new. The nine arrangers bring to this volume the fruits of their different backgrounds and musical experiences. Joseph Jennings, conductor, singer, and arranger, and Steve Barnett, pianist, arranger, and record producer, are both from the United States. Lydia Adams is conductor of the Elmer Iseler Singers and the Amadeus Choir in Toronto, and Jon Washburn is the founder and conductor of the Vancouver Chamber Choir. Péter Louis van Dijk is a flourishing composer from Cape Town. Paul Hart and Andrew Pryce Jackman are two of Britain's most successful 'commercial' composers. Also from Britain, are singer and composer Roderick Williams, the editor, pianist, and arranger David Blackwell, and me.

I hope that this collection will inspire performers to sing with all their heart, and celebrate the joy, the depth of feeling, and the reverence that these songs inspire.

Bob Chilcott

for Norman Morris and the Reading Phoenix Choir

1. All my trials

arr. BOB CHILCOTT

2. Balm in Gilead

arr. JON WASHBURN

BARITONE (or MEZZO SOPRANO) SOLO

Solo: Some-times I feel dis-cour-aged and think my work in vain,
but then the Ho-ly Spi-rit re-vives my soul a-gain.

S.: mm,
A.: mm
T.: mm
B.: mm

re-vives a-gain. O
re-vives my soul a-gain. O
Oh re-vives a-gain. O
re-vives my soul a-gain.
Oh re-vives a-gain.

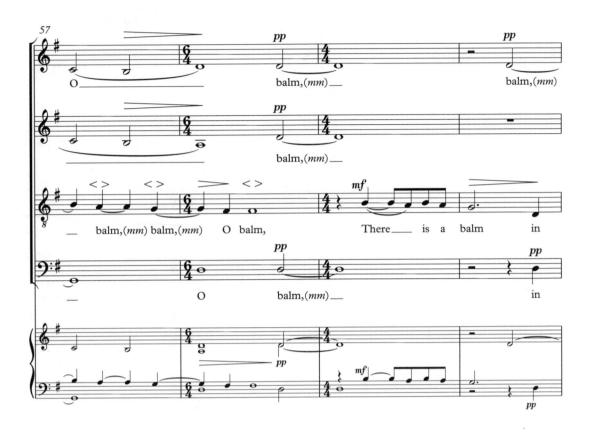

for Marjukka Riihimäki and Grex Musicus

3. By and by

arr. BOB CHILCOTT

hell___ is___ deep___ and a dark des - pair,___

Hell___ is deep___ and a dark des - pair,___

Hell___ is deep___ and a dark___ des - pair, oh___

Hell is deep___ and a dark des - pair,

I'm gon - na lay down my hea - vy___ load. O

I'm gon - na lay down my hea - vy load.___

I'm gon - na lay down my hea - vy load.___

I'm gon - na lay down my hea - vy load.___

I'm gon-na lay down my hea-vy, hea-vy load._____

I'm gon-na lay down hea - vy

4. Deep river

arr. PAUL HART

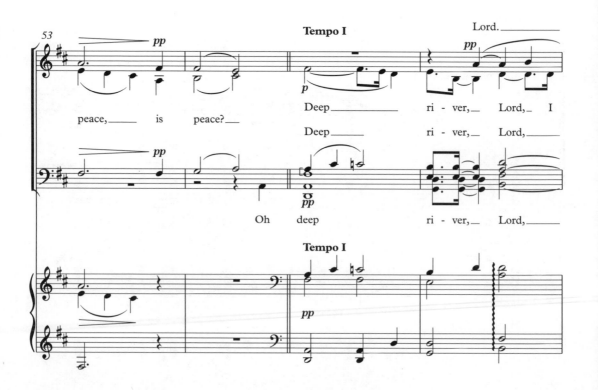

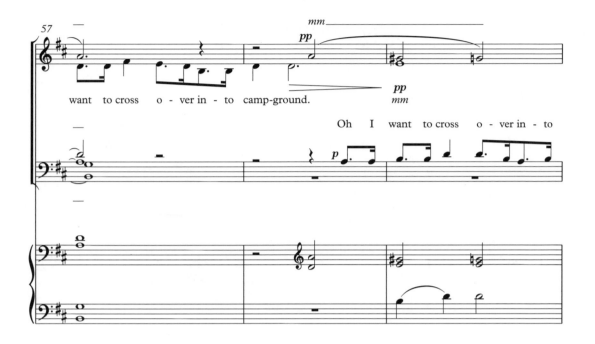

for Jennifer Tham and the Singapore Youth Choir

5. Didn't it rain

arr. BOB CHILCOTT

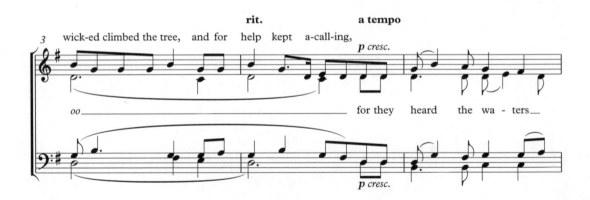

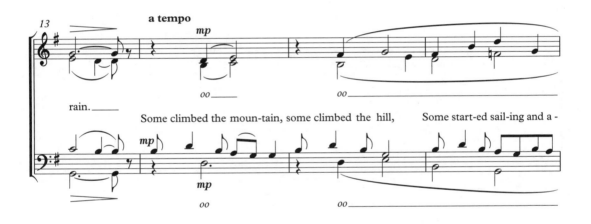

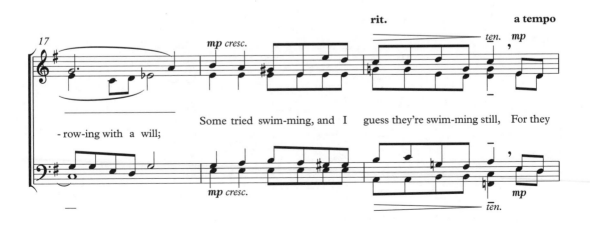

heard   the   wa - ters   roar - ing,   Did-n't it___   rain,_____

rain,_____   didn't   it   rain,_____   No - ah,___

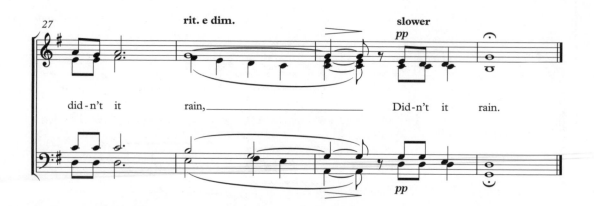

did-n't   it   rain,_____   Did-n't   it   rain.

6. Didn't my Lord deliver Daniel?

arr. PAUL HART

why not - a ev - e - ry man? De win' blow eas' an' de

win' blow wes', It blow like de judge - ment day, An'

ev - 'ry poor soul_ that ne - ver did pray_ Will be glad to pray_ that

for Sheila Harrod and the Kentwood Choir

7. Ev'ry time I feel the Spirit

arr. BOB CHILCOTT

I will pray.   Ain't but one train____

on this track,_____ runs to hea - ven

and right back.   Saint Pe - ter wait - ing____

for Louis Botto – creator and former artistic director of Chanticleer,
and for all those who have left us much too soon

8. Goin' home to God

arr. STEVE BARNETT

* All asterisked sections if too high for all basses may be performed by a) all basses in falsetto returning to 'normal' voice where comfortable; or b) baritones only with basses joining subtly in the next bar.

home   to   God,_____   to   God.

home   to   God,_____   to   God.

home   to   God,   go - in'_   home   to_____   to   God.

home   to   God,   go - in'_   home   to_____   God,   to   God.

home   to   God,_____   to_____   God.

9. Go tell it on the mountains

arr. PÉTER LOUIS VAN DIJK

*open mouth slightly.

Quasi alla marcia (come prima) ma intenso

Soprano 1 and Tenor 1 should be taken by a small sub group here.

10. I got a robe

arr. RODERICK WILLIAMS

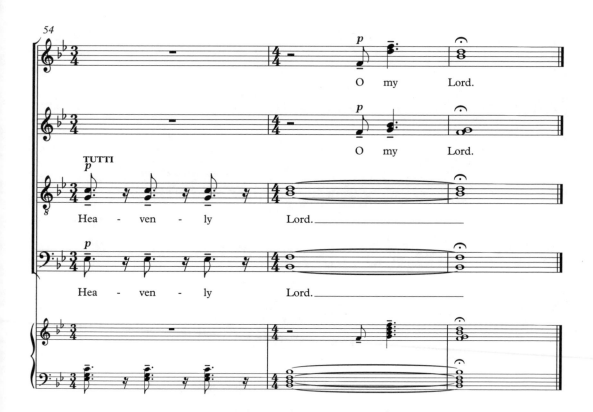

11. I want Jesus to walk with me

arr. RODERICK WILLIAMS

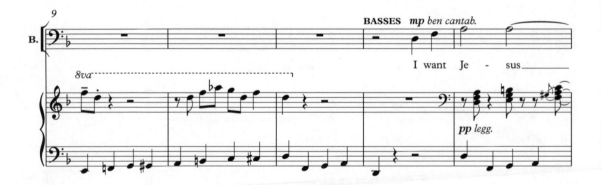

* The bass line of the piano part may also be augmented by a double bass playing pizzicato.

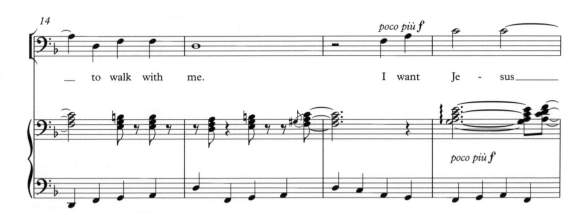

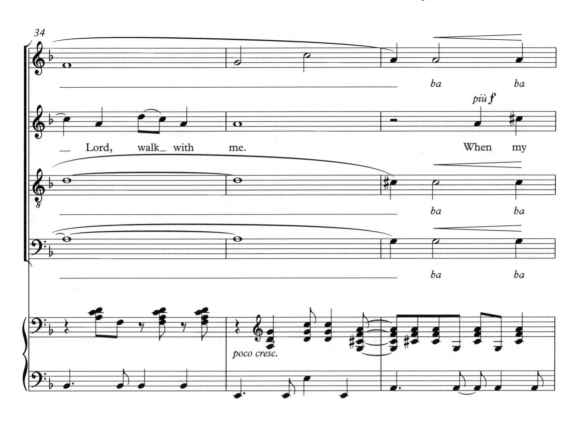

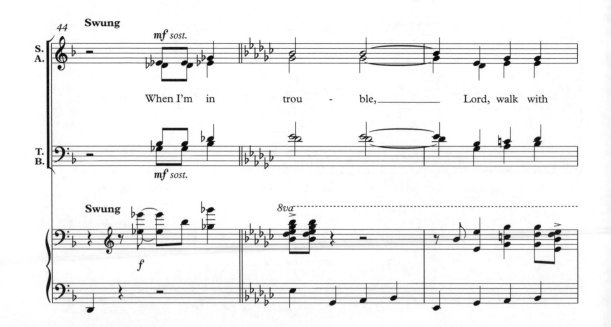

* Altos and basses can miss out the top note and join on the 'E'.

12. Joshua fit the battle of Jericho

arr. STEVE BARNETT

for Karen Grylls and the Tower New Zealand Youth Choir

13. Nobody knows the trouble I've seen

arr. BOB CHILCOTT

Glo - ry hal - le - lu - ia!

T. or B. SOLO
Al-though you see____ me____ going a - long,____

S.
A.
oo ____

T.
B.

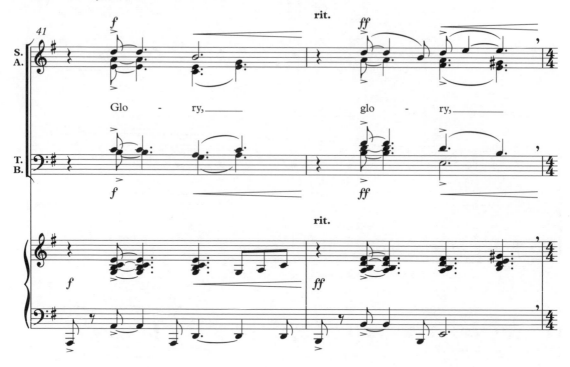

14. Peter, go ring them bells

arr. RODERICK WILLIAMS

* The solo can be sung at this pitch by a tenor or a strong-voiced mezzo/contralto; alternatively it can be sung an octave higher by a soprano. The solo part is freely notated and should be improvised as much as possible.

15. Steal away

arr. DAVID BLACKWELL

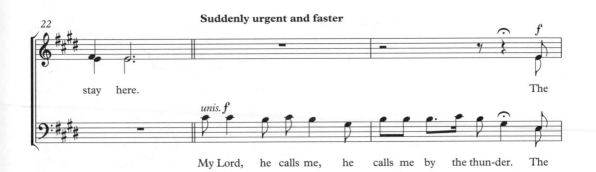

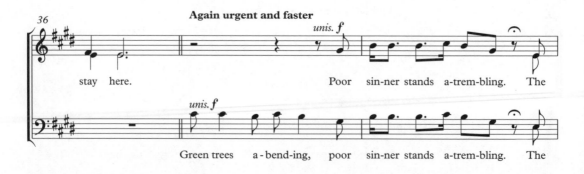

16. Surely He died on Calvary

arr. JOSEPH JENNINGS

*Keyboard reduction for rehearsal only.

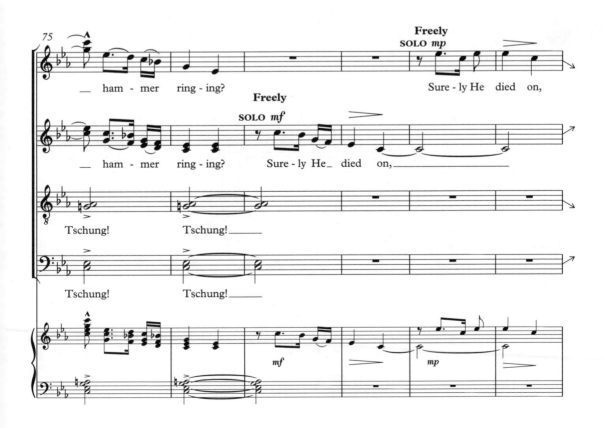

17. Swing low, sweet chariot

arr. ANDREW PRYCE JACKMAN

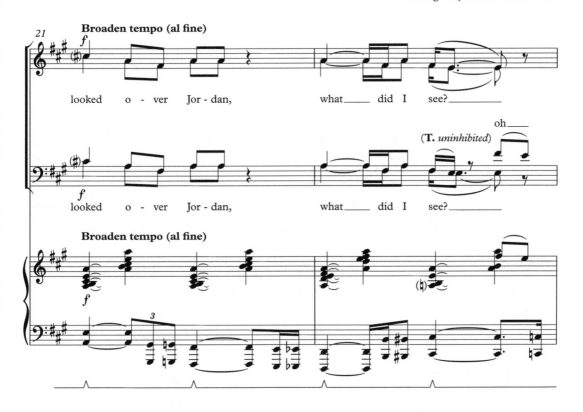

Hushed and ecstatic

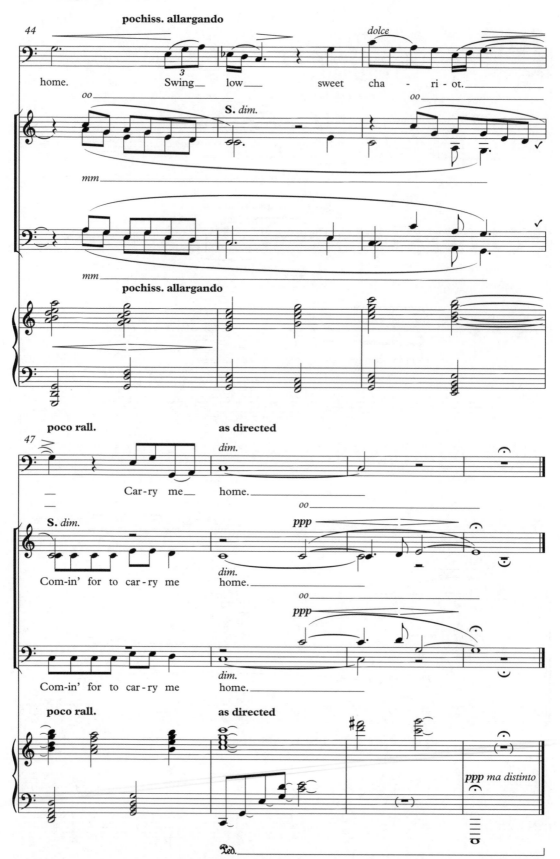

in joyful memory of Barbara McCaw Hull

18. Wade in the water

arr. LYDIA ADAMS
piano CYNTHIA DAVIES

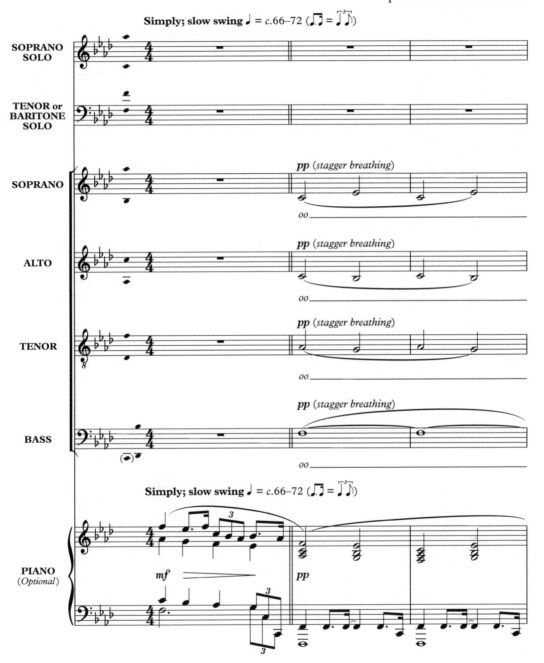

*A cool 'jazz' sound, without vibrato.

19. Way over in Beulah-lan'

arr. JOSEPH JENNINGS

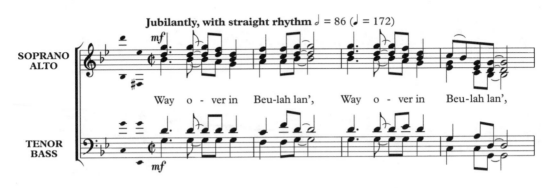

we gon - na drink   of that   Ho - ly wine, ___

Oh,   my Lor-dy, Lor-dy,   oh,   my Lor-dy, Lor-dy,   Way   o - ver in

dm   *dm   dm*

Beu - lah lan'.   I said   way   o - ver in   Beu - lah lan',   Way   o - ver in

Beu - lah lan', ___   We gon - na have   a   good   time _____

___   Way o-ver in   Beu - lah lan'. I said   way   o - ver in   Beu - lah lan', Oh child-ren

SOLI

SOLI

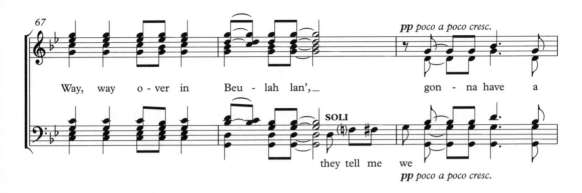

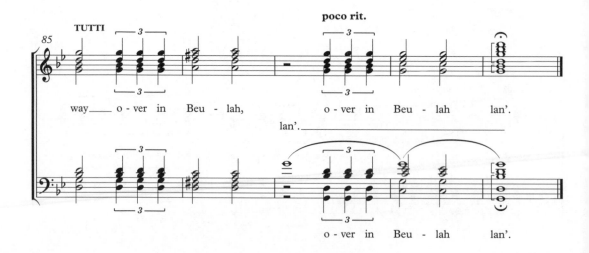

20. Were you there?

arr. PAUL HART